extra easy
meals in
minutes

Welcome

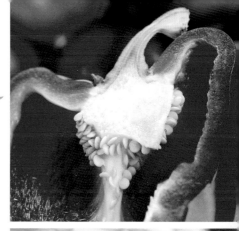

If you're short on time and still want to enjoy delicious, satisfying and nutritious food – then you'll love the **Extra Easy Meals in Minutes** cookbook. It's a collection of over 50 hassle-free recipes that you can put on the table in 30 minutes or less.

Whether you want to whizz up a family supper, grab a speedy snack or entertain friends without spending hours in the kitchen, we've catered for every occasion. From curry in a hurry and fish in a flash to faster pasta and super-quick stir-fries, you can relax knowing that all these time-saving recipes are kind to your waistline – and to your pocket too!

This nifty book is bursting with practical information to make it even easier to decide what to cook when you're in a hurry, and it features loads of top tips to help you get the best out of what you're making, and to adapt recipes to suit your own tastes.

It doesn't matter if you're a beginner or a masterchef in the kitchen, you'll find these super-filling, super-fast recipes extremely easy to follow.

So forget expensive takeaways – all the tasty recipes in this book are completely Free or low in Syns so you can enjoy fast food that's good for you without ever feeling hungry!

Extra Easy Meals in Minutes is split into 5 chapters…

Light bites

These recipes are fantastic
for a light lunch, brunch,
speedy snack or starter.

caldo verde

1 garlic clove, peeled and crushed

1 small onion, peeled and finely chopped

150g shredded spring greens or cabbage

1 carrot, peeled and finely diced

300g Desirée potatoes, peeled and cut into 1.5cm cubes

800ml vegetable stock

2 tsp each of dried coriander and mint

1 tsp dried thyme

400g can cannellini beans, undrained

salt and freshly ground black pepper

Basic but delicious, this rustic Portuguese broth is bursting with fresh flavours and textures.

A classic recipe made with simple storecupboard staples, this healthy and hearty vegetable soup is easy on the pocket, quick to prepare and makes for a satisfying starter or wholesome light lunch.

Place all the ingredients (except for the beans and seasoning) in a medium-sized saucepan and bring to the boil.

Reduce the heat to medium, cover and cook for 10-12 minutes or until the potatoes and vegetables are just tender.

Stir in the beans and bring back to the boil. Cook for 2-3 minutes and remove from the heat.

Season well and serve immediately.

Create a filling main course in a flash by stirring in cooked rice.

chicken and vegetable soup

serves 4

Free

ready in 25 minutes

2 onions, peeled and sliced

2 celery sticks,
roughly chopped

2 carrots, peeled and cut
into bite-sized pieces

2 medium potatoes,
peeled and cut into
bite-sized pieces

1.2 litres chicken stock

300g cooked skinless chicken
breast, roughly shredded

1 tbsp finely chopped fresh
flat-leaf parsley

salt and freshly ground
black pepper

There's nothing like warming chicken soup to make you feel good. And this one is packed with fresh veg, so you can feel good about that too!

As well as nourishing body and soul, this classic, comforting soup will make the most of leftover poached or roasted chicken and any root vegetables.

Place the onions, celery, carrots, potatoes and stock in a saucepan and bring to the boil.

Reduce the heat to medium, cover and cook for 12-15 minutes or until the vegetables are tender.

Add the cooked chicken and parsley, season well and cook until heated through.

Serve immediately.

warm beef and rice noodle salad

serves 4

Free

ready in under 20 minutes

4 tbsp light soy sauce

1 level tsp sweet chilli sauce

juice of 1 lime

1 tsp Thai fish sauce (nam pla)

¼ tsp sweetener

200g dried stir-fry rice noodles

8 spring onions, cut into 2cm diagonal lengths

1 red pepper, deseeded and cut into very thin strips

½ cucumber, shredded or cut into thin matchsticks

200g cooked roast beef slices, visible fat removed, cut into thin strips

Thinly sliced cooked beef and a medley of colourful vegetables mingle with oodles of rice noodles in this Asian-inspired salad.

Simple and super-quick to prepare, this light and elegant dish explodes with flavours and makes the perfect start to a meal or a delicious light lunch, hot or cold.

Mix together the soy sauce, sweet chilli sauce, lime juice, fish sauce and sweetener in a bowl and set aside.

Meanwhile, place the rice noodles in a bowl of boiling hot water and leave to soak for 7-8 minutes. Drain well and put the drained noodles onto a wide serving platter.

Add the vegetables and the beef strips and pour over the soy dressing. Toss to mix well and serve immediately or at room temperature.

piri piri chicken
and vegetable skewers

These skewers promise to spice up any mealtime!
To save preparation time, and to ensure each chunk
of chicken is tender and full of flavour, marinate the
meat the night before. For an Indian twist substitute
the piri piri seasoning for curry powder.

serves 4

Free

ready in 20 minutes

800g skinless and boneless
chicken breasts, cut into
bite-sized pieces

2 tbsp piri piri seasoning

juice of 2 limes

salt and freshly ground
black pepper

1 large courgette,
cut into thick slices

24 cherry tomatoes

lime wedges, to serve

Preheat the grill to medium-hot. Place the chicken pieces in a large
ceramic bowl.

Mix the piri piri seasoning and lime juice together in a small bowl. Season
well and pour this mixture over the chicken. Toss to coat evenly.

Thread the chicken pieces onto eight metal skewers, alternating with courgette
slices and cherry tomatoes. Cook under the grill for 4-5 minutes on each side
or until the edges of the chicken and vegetables are lightly charred in places
and the chicken is cooked through.

Serve with wedges of lime to squeeze over.

thai-style chicken cakes

serves 4 (makes 12)

Free

ready in under 25 minutes

4 large, skinless and
boneless chicken breasts,
roughly chopped

2 garlic cloves,
peeled and crushed

1 tsp grated root ginger

6 spring onions,
finely chopped

small pack fresh coriander
(leaves and stems), chopped

2 tbsp finely chopped
fresh mint

1 tbsp finely chopped
lemon grass

finely grated zest
and juice of 1 lime

1 red chilli, deseeded
and chopped

salt and freshly ground
black pepper

low calorie cooking spray

for the salad

1 large cucumber

1 large carrot

1 small red onion, thinly sliced

juice of 1 large lemon

For the ultimate taste sensation serve these tasty cakes with sweet chilli sauce (1½ Syns per level tablespoon).

Mini versions work well at parties served on cocktail sticks, while a larger version makes a great burger.

Preheat the oven to 220°C/Fan 200°C/Gas 7.

Place the chicken, garlic, ginger, spring onions, coriander, mint, lemon grass, lime zest and juice and red chilli into a food processor and season well. Blitz until the chicken is finely ground and everything is well mixed. Divide the mixture into 12 portions and, using your hands, shape into small cakes.

Spray a large non-stick frying pan with low calorie cooking spray, and fry the cakes over a medium heat for 3-4 minutes, turning once. Transfer to a non-stick baking sheet and place in the preheated oven for 6-8 minutes.

Meanwhile, make the salad by peeling the cucumber and carrots into thin ribbons, using a vegetable peeler or mandolin, and place in a bowl with the sliced red onion and the lemon juice. Season well and set aside.

Remove the cakes from the oven and serve immediately with the cucumber salad.

Swap the chicken breasts for 500g lean turkey mince (5% fat or less) if you prefer.

pan-seared
scallop salad

Soft and fleshy in texture and delicately sweet in flavour, scallops are a real treat any night of the week.

This zingy salad of juicy pan-seared scallops with potatoes, vegetables and herbs makes for a mouth-watering starter or it can be served as part of a delicious mixed salad buffet.

Place the potatoes in a large pan of lightly salted water and boil for 8-10 minutes or until just tender. Remove from the heat, drain thoroughly and set aside.

Place the lime juice and lemon juice in a food processor with the stock, garlic, chillies, sweetener and chopped coriander. Process until fairly smooth then transfer to a bowl.

Spray a large non-stick frying pan with low calorie cooking spray and place over a high heat. Add the drained potatoes and stir-fry for 4-5 minutes or until lightly browned. Transfer to a wide bowl, cover and keep warm.

Spray a griddle with low calorie cooking spray and place over a high heat. Add the scallops and cook for 1-2 minutes on each side or until just cooked through (don't overcook them or they will turn rubbery).

Add the scallops to the potatoes, along with the spring onions, cucumber and peppers.

Add the lime juice mixture, toss to mix well and serve immediately.

serves 4

Free

ready in under 25 minutes

300g new potatoes, peeled and cut into 1.5cm dice

juice of 4 limes

juice of 1 lemon

50ml vegetable stock

2 garlic cloves, peeled and crushed

2 jalapeno chillies, deseeded and finely chopped

1 tsp sweetener

40g finely chopped fresh coriander

low calorie cooking spray

20 king scallops, cleaned and rinsed

8 spring onions, cut into 2cm lengths

½ cucumber, finely diced

1 red pepper, deseeded and finely diced

1 yellow pepper, deseeded and finely diced

hot smoked trout
and dill pâté

serves 4

Free

ready in 15 minutes

4 x 150g hot smoked trout
fillets, skinned and flaked

125g low fat
natural cottage cheese

150g quark

juice of ½ lime

2 tbsp finely chopped
cornichons or gherkins

1 tbsp capers

2 tbsp finely chopped bottled
roasted red peppers

4 tbsp finely chopped
fresh dill

salt and freshly ground
black pepper

vegetable crudités,
to serve (carrot, celery,
cucumber and peppers)

This creamy trout pâté with capers and fresh dill makes an easy starter or lunchtime snack. It's great to take on a picnic or as a packed lunch served with vegetable crudités.

Place the trout in a food processor with the cottage cheese, quark, lime juice, cornichons or gherkins, capers, roasted red peppers and dill. Season well and blend until smooth.

Spoon the mixture into four individual ramekins or one small to medium-sized bowl.

This pâté can be chilled overnight before serving or it can be served immediately with vegetable crudités of your choice.

> You can use smoked salmon,
> hot smoked salmon or mackerel
> for a tasty alternative.

warm hake and rigatoni salad

If you love fish, you'll fall hook, line and sinker for this delicious warm salad.

Bursting with lovely textures, flavours and colours, it guarantees to bring a little Mediterranean sunshine to the table!

serves 4
Free
ready in 15 minutes

Cook the pasta according to the packet instructions. Drain and keep warm.

Meanwhile, spray a large non-stick frying pan with low calorie cooking spray and place over a high heat.

Add the garlic, tomatoes, passata, yellow pepper, red chilli flakes and oregano and bring to the boil.

Reduce the heat to medium, add the hake cubes and gently toss in the tomato mixture. Cover and simmer for 2-3 minutes or until the fish is cooked through. Season well.

Place the pasta in a wide serving bowl and carefully spoon over the tomato and fish sauce. Gently toss to mix well, sprinkle over the parsley and serve warm or at room temperature.

200g dried rigatoni pasta

low calorie cooking spray

2 garlic cloves, peeled and finely chopped

100g ripe tomatoes, roughly chopped

200g passata with onions and garlic

1 yellow pepper, deseeded and cut into 1.5cm pieces

a pinch of dried red chilli flakes

1 tsp dried oregano

250g skinless hake fillets, cut into bite-sized cubes

salt and freshly ground black pepper

4 tbsp finely chopped fresh flat-leaf parsley, to garnish

Swap the hake for 250g cooked and peeled prawns if you fancy a change.

smoked salmon, cottage cheese and rocket rolls

serves 4 (makes 16)

Free

ready in 15 minutes

4 tbsp low fat natural cottage cheese

2 tbsp quark

1 tsp lemon juice

2 tbsp finely chopped fresh dill

freshly ground black pepper

16 smoked salmon strips (about 12 x 4cm each)

75g wild rocket leaves

lemon wedges, to serve

These canapés are really easy to assemble, pretty to look at and delicious to eat.

They make great party food or are delicious served as a light starter.

Mix the cottage cheese, quark, lemon juice and chopped dill together in a bowl. Season with freshly ground black pepper.

Lay half of the salmon strips on a work surface and divide half of the cottage cheese mixture along the length of each strip, leaving a 2cm border at one short end.

Top with some of the rocket and roll up tightly into a neat roll. Repeat to make 16 rolls.

Sprinkle over some freshly ground black pepper and serve immediately with lemon wedges.

cheesy garlic and herb stuffed mushrooms

Take the humble mushroom, dress it up just a little – and turn it into a show-stopping starter. Stuffed with cottage cheese and herbs then grilled until golden, these mouth-watering mushrooms are so quick and easy to prepare!

Preheat the grill to medium-high. Trim and remove the mushroom stalks and finely chop them.

Spray a non-stick frying pan with low calorie cooking spray. Add the chopped mushroom stalks, spring onions and one crushed garlic clove and stir-fry over a high heat for 6-8 minutes.

Season well and transfer to a bowl with the remaining garlic cloves, the cottage cheese, lemon zest and chopped herbs.

Place the mushroom caps, gill side up, on a grill rack in a single layer and season well. Divide the stuffing among the caps and sprinkle with the Parmesan. Place the grill rack about 12cm from the heat and cook for 6-8 minutes or until the tops are golden and bubbling.

Divide the spinach leaves between four plates, top each with two stuffed mushrooms and serve immediately, garnished with the pink peppercorns and chopped chives.

serves 4

1 Syn per serving

ready in under 25 minutes

8 large flat field or Portobello mushrooms

low calorie cooking spray

4 spring onions, finely chopped

3 garlic cloves, peeled and crushed

salt and freshly ground black pepper

200g low fat natural cottage cheese

1 tbsp finely grated unwaxed lemon zest

1 tbsp finely chopped fresh chives

2 tbsp finely chopped fresh flat-leaf parsley

4 level tbsp freshly grated Parmesan cheese

50g baby leaf spinach

crushed pink peppercorns and finely chopped fresh chives, to garnish

Swap the cottage cheese for quark if you prefer — the mushrooms will wear it equally well.

chickpea and chilli cakes with minted yogurt dip

serves 4 (makes 20)

3 Syns per serving

ready in under 25 minutes

2 x 400g cans chickpeas, drained

1 tsp ground cumin

4 slices medium bread from a small 400g wholemeal loaf, made into breadcrumbs

3 eggs, beaten

8 tbsp of finely chopped fresh coriander

1 red chilli, deseeded and finely chopped

4 spring onions, finely chopped

low calorie cooking spray

for the dip

150g fat free natural yogurt

4-5 tbsp very finely chopped fresh mint

a pinch each of ground cumin and ground cinnamon

salt and freshly ground black pepper

These moreish vegetarian patties have a slightly spicy flavour so taste delicious with a cool, refreshing minted yogurt dip.

Make them small and they're the perfect canapé, medium-sized and they're a tasty vegetarian starter or light lunch, go a bit bigger and you have a fabulously filling meat-free alternative to a burger.

First make the dip by mixing all the dip ingredients together in a bowl. Season well, cover and chill until needed.

Place the chickpeas, cumin, breadcrumbs, egg, coriander, red chilli and spring onions in a food processor and blend until fairly smooth. Transfer to a mixing bowl and season well.

Spray a large non-stick frying pan with low calorie cooking spray and place over a medium-high heat. Working in batches, drop large tablespoons of the batter onto the pan (spacing them apart) and lightly press down to form a 'cake' or 'patty' shape.

Cook for 2-3 minutes on each side or until lightly browned and cooked through. Repeat with the remaining chickpea mixture.

Serve the chickpea cakes with the yogurt dip.

The kids will love helping you make these. If they're going to help you eat them too, you may want to leave out the chilli or use a mild variety.

Faster pasta, rice & grains

Filling, comforting meals
featuring pasta, rice,
couscous and pulses.

creamy ham
and artichoke tagliatelle

serves 4

Free

ready in under 20 minutes

350g dried tagliatelle

200g sugar snap peas, trimmed

1 egg, beaten

150g fat free natural fromage frais

2 tbsp finely chopped fresh tarragon

2 garlic cloves, peeled and crushed

salt and freshly ground black pepper

low calorie cooking spray

350g lean ham, cut into bite-sized cubes

400g can artichoke hearts in water, drained and halved

Get your week off to a great start with this satisfying pasta dish. It's so simple to make yet it looks and tastes impressive.

If you're not an artichoke fan, asparagus would work just as well.

Cook the pasta according to the packet instructions, adding the sugar snap peas for the last 3 minutes of cooking time.

Meanwhile, whisk together the egg, fromage frais, chopped tarragon and garlic. Season well and set aside.

Spray a large non-stick frying pan with low calorie cooking spray, add the ham and artichokes and stir-fry for 2-3 minutes or until heated through.

Drain the pasta and peas and add to the frying pan along with the fromage frais mixture. Toss to mix well and serve immediately.

For a veggie alternative, substitute the ham for 200g drained and chopped, bottled roasted red peppers. Add them at the same time as the artichokes.

gingered turkey noodles

serves 4

1 Syn per serving

ready in under 30 minutes

250g dried egg noodles

low calorie cooking spray

500g skinless turkey breast steaks, cut into thin strips

2 carrots, peeled and cut into thin sticks

1 red pepper, deseeded and sliced

150g broccoli florets

250g baby sweetcorn, halved lengthways

250g mangetout, halved lengthways

2 tsp grated root ginger

1 garlic clove, peeled and crushed

100ml chicken stock

2 level tbsp sweet chilli sauce

2 tbsp soy sauce

Turn turkey into something special with this Oriental-style noodle stir-fry. Boasting a vibrant mix of vegetables and intense ginger and garlic flavours, it's a real taste sensation.

The secret to a good stir-fry is to have everything prepped and ready before you start cooking. Then you can throw your ingredients in one after the other and you'll have a meal in minutes!

Prepare the noodles according to the packet instructions, drain and keep warm.

Spray a large non-stick wok or frying pan with low calorie cooking spray and place over a medium-high heat. Add the turkey and stir-fry for 6-8 minutes or until sealed and cooked through.

Add the carrots, red pepper and broccoli and stir-fry for 4 minutes.

Add the baby sweetcorn to the wok along with the mangetout, ginger and garlic. Stir-fry for 3-4 minutes.

Finally add the drained noodles, the stock, sweet chilli sauce and soy sauce and mix well.

Heat until piping hot and serve immediately.

Fresh root ginger stores really well in the freezer. Simply peel, chop into chunks and wrap in cling film. You'll find frozen ginger grates easily too!

linguine with creamy pesto sauce

serves 4
2½ Syns per serving
ready in under 20 minutes

350g dried linguine

350g green beans,
trimmed and halved

for the pesto sauce

50g fresh basil,
roughly chopped

25g rocket leaves,
roughly chopped

50g freshly grated Parmesan
cheese or Pecorino cheese,
plus extra to serve (optional)

2-3 garlic cloves, peeled

150g fat free natural
fromage frais

100ml vegetable stock

Make this no-fuss pasta dish your dish of the day. Whether you need a quick midweek meal or fancy something tasty for the weekend, this promises to be a firm favourite with family and friends.

The pesto sauce is also terrific drizzled over cooked potatoes or meat, especially chicken.

Cook the pasta according to the packet instructions, adding the green beans to the pan for the last 3 minutes of cooking time.

Meanwhile, make the pesto by placing the basil and rocket leaves in a food processor with the grated cheese and the garlic. Blend until everything is finely chopped. Scrape down the sides of the bowl with a spatula and ensure there are no large chunks remaining – if there are, blend again briefly.

Add the fromage frais and stock to the processor and blitz again until creamy and fairly smooth.

Drain the pasta and beans and return to the saucepan. Stir in the pesto sauce and toss to mix well.

Serve immediately garnished with a little extra grated Parmesan (1 Syn per level tablespoon).

The pesto sauce can be prepared up to a week in advance. Cover and chill in the fridge until ready to use. For a spicy version, add one chopped green chilli to the pesto mix.

pasta with prawns, chilli and tomatoes

Pep up plain pasta with this scrumptious and speedy seafood sauce packed with juicy prawns.

If you're not a fan of prawns, use canned crab meat instead. Simply toss the crab meat with the rocket and serve.

Cook the pasta according to the packet instructions. Drain and set aside.

Spray a deep frying pan or wok with low calorie cooking spray and place over a high heat.

Add the garlic, tomatoes and red chillies, season well, add the prawns and heat through. Then add the drained pasta.

Remove from the heat, fold through the rocket and stir to mix well. Serve immediately with a crisp salad, if you like.

serves 4

Free

ready in 15-20 minutes

400g dried short-shaped pasta

low calorie cooking spray

2 garlic cloves, peeled and finely chopped

2 ripe plum tomatoes, finely chopped

2 long red chillies, deseeded (optional) and diced

salt and freshly ground black pepper

400g cooked and peeled tiger prawns

2 x 70g bags wild rocket

a crisp salad, to serve (optional)

For a quick and simple vegetarian option, simply omit the prawns and double the quantity of tomatoes.

tuna
penne niçoise

serves 4

½ **Syn** per serving

ready in under 20 minutes

Packed with pasta, tuna and boiled eggs, this salad makes a really hearty meal and is sure to keep you feeling fuller for longer. It also works well as a packed lunch or for a picnic.

200g dried penne

200g green beans, trimmed and halved

2 x 185g cans tuna chunks in spring water, drained

2 little gem lettuce, leaves separated and roughly torn into bite-sized pieces

1 yellow pepper, deseeded and cut into small pieces

200g midi or large cherry tomatoes, halved or quartered

8 pitted black olives

1 red onion, peeled and thinly sliced

4 eggs, boiled to your liking, halved or quartered* (optional)

for the dressing

6 tbsp fat free vinaigrette

juice of 1 lemon

1 level tsp wholegrain mustard

salt and freshly ground black pepper

Pregnant women, the elderly and babies are advised not to eat raw or partially cooked eggs.

Cook the pasta according to the packet instructions, adding the green beans to the pan for the last 3 minutes of cooking time.

Place the tuna, lettuce, yellow pepper, tomatoes, olives and red onion in a wide bowl.

Make the dressing by whisking all the ingredients together. Season well.

Drain the pasta and the beans and add to the tuna mixture. Pour over the dressing and toss gently to mix well.

Garnish each serving with a boiled egg, if using, and serve immediately.

black-eyed bean and vegetable chilli bowl

Heat up the kitchen with a satisfyingly spicy vegetarian chilli that your whole family will love.

This dish freezes really well. Make up a huge batch, split into smaller portions and freeze for up to a month.

serves 4
Free
❄ Ⓥ
ready in under 25 minutes

Spray a large frying pan with low calorie cooking spray and place over a medium heat.

Add the shallots, garlic, celery, carrots and red pepper and stir-fry for 2-3 minutes.

Add the dried herbs, ground cumin, ground cinnamon, chilli powder, tomatoes and stock and bring to the boil.

Reduce the heat, cover and allow to cook gently for 10-12 minutes or until the vegetables are tender.

Stir in the beans and cook for 2-3 minutes or until piping hot.

Season well, remove from the heat and sprinkle over the coriander.

Serve with cooked rice and lime wedges to squeeze over.

low calorie cooking spray

4 shallots, peeled and finely chopped

2 garlic cloves, peeled and crushed

2 celery sticks, cut into 1.5cm dice

1 large carrot, peeled and cut into 1.5cm pieces

1 red pepper, deseeded and cut into 1.5cm pieces

1 tsp each of dried mixed herbs, ground cumin, ground cinnamon and chilli powder

400g can chopped tomatoes

200ml vegetable stock

400g can black-eyed beans in water, drained

400g can red kidney beans in chilli sauce

salt and freshly ground black pepper

4 tbsp finely chopped fresh coriander leaves

lime wedges, to serve

Serve with extra Speed vegetables
instead of rice to make this
a perfect **Extra Easy** meal.

herbed minced beef
and vegetable couscous

serves 4

Free

ready in under 20 minutes

200g dried couscous

300ml boiling hot
vegetable stock

low calorie cooking spray

250g lean beef mince
(5% fat or less)

1 red pepper, deseeded
and finely chopped

1 carrot, peeled
and finely diced

100g green beans,
cut into 1.5cm lengths

1 tsp ground cumin

1 tsp curry powder

salt and freshly ground
black pepper

2 tbsp each of finely chopped
fresh mint and coriander

1 tomato, finely chopped

4 tbsp fat free natural yogurt,
sprinkled with smoked
paprika, to serve

You won't have to be in the kitchen for long with this deliciously speedy Moroccan-inspired recipe.

Bringing a rainbow of colour to the table, this satisfying after-work supper will help you on your way to five a day – and another great week on the scales!

Place the couscous in a wide heat-resistant bowl and pour over the boiling hot stock. Cover with cling film and leave to soak for 10-12 minutes.

Meanwhile, spray a large non-stick frying pan with low calorie cooking spray and place over a high heat. Add the mince and vegetables and stir-fry for 8-10 minutes or until sealed and cooked through.

Add the ground cumin and curry powder and stir-fry for 1-2 minutes. Remove from the heat, season and keep warm.

Fluff up the grains of the couscous with a fork and place the mixture in a wide serving bowl. Add the beef, chopped herbs and tomatoes and toss to mix well. Serve immediately with a spoonful of fat free natural yogurt, sprinkled with smoked paprika.

This tasty and flavoursome dish can be eaten warm or at room temperature, making it an ideal lunchbox filler too.

speedy vegetable
and chicken rice

With this tried, tested and trusted fried rice recipe to hand you'll never be tempted by takeaway again!

Big on taste and small on Syns, it's a great way to use up leftover rice (if you don't have any to use up, cook some as you prepare all your other ingredients).

Spray a large non-stick frying pan or wok with low calorie cooking spray and place over a medium-high heat. Add the garlic, ginger and stir-fry vegetables and stir-fry for 4-5 minutes.

Turn the heat to high and stir in the cooked rice and shredded chicken. Stir-fry for 3-4 minutes or until piping hot.

Add the soy sauce, stir-fry for 30 seconds and then drizzle over the beaten egg. Cook for 2-3 minutes or until the egg has scrambled.

Remove from the heat and stir in the spring onions. Serve immediately garnished with spring onion slivers.

serves 4

Free

ready in under 20 minutes

low calorie cooking spray

2 garlic cloves, peeled and crushed or grated

1 tsp grated root ginger

300g pack crunchy stir-fry vegetables

425g cold, cooked white long grain rice

400g cooked, skinless chicken breast, roughly shredded

4 tbsp light soy sauce

2 eggs, lightly beaten

6 spring onions, finely sliced

spring onion slivers, to garnish

This recipe also works well with basmati rice.

chickpea and roasted red pepper pilaf

serves 4

2½ Syns per serving

ready in under 20 minutes
plus standing

low calorie cooking spray

1 red onion, peeled and
finely chopped

1 garlic clove, peeled
and crushed

1 tsp ground cumin

1 tsp ground cinnamon

175g dried bulgar wheat

350ml vegetable stock

200g bottled roasted red
peppers, drained and
roughly chopped

400g can chickpeas, drained

small pack fresh dill,
finely chopped

small pack fresh flat-leaf
parsley, finely chopped

2 tbsp finely chopped
fresh mint

110g reduced fat feta cheese,
roughly chopped or crumbled

salt and freshly ground
black pepper

Keep the washing-up to an absolute minimum with this healthy one-pot supper!

In this recipe traditional pilaf gets a new lease of life with the addition of chickpeas, creating a dish that's filling and full of flavour.

This is comfort food at its best and once you've mastered it, why not experiment with different vegetables and spices for new taste sensations?

Spray a heavy-based saucepan with low calorie cooking spray and add the onion, garlic, ground cumin, ground cinnamon and bulgar wheat. Place over a medium heat and cook, stirring, for 1-2 minutes to lightly toast the grains.

Pour the stock into the saucepan, stir well, then bring to the boil. Cover, reduce the heat and cook on a gentle simmer for 6-8 minutes or until all the liquid is absorbed.

Remove from the heat and add the red peppers and chickpeas, without stirring them in. Cover and allow to stand for 15 minutes.

Just before serving, remove the lid from the pilaf and fluff up the grains with a fork, mixing in the red pepper and chickpeas. Carefully fold in the chopped herbs and scatter over the feta cheese.

Season to taste and serve hot, warm or cold.

If you prefer, you can swap the bulgar wheat for couscous or replace the chickpeas with canned mixed beans.

Meaty mains

Mouth-watering meat and poultry dishes the whole family will love.

minced beef hash

A modern twist on traditional corned beef hash, this is good, simple food at its best.

Cheap, cheerful and extremely comforting, it uses ingredients you'll find in your cupboard and it's really easy to rustle up for a quick dinner.

serves 4

Free

ready in under 30 minutes

low calorie cooking spray

2 onions, peeled and finely chopped

2 garlic cloves, peeled and crushed

1 tsp ground cumin

1 green chilli, deseeded and finely diced

450g lean beef mince (5% fat or less)

1 carrot, peeled and diced

300g potatoes, peeled and diced

400g can plum tomatoes

100ml beef stock

1 tsp dried oregano

4 tbsp roughly chopped fresh flat-leaf parsley

salt and freshly ground black pepper

Spray a large frying pan with low calorie cooking spray and place over a medium heat. Add the onions and stir-fry for 2-3 minutes.

Add the garlic, cumin and green chilli, stirring for a few moments to release the flavours.

Add the minced beef and cook on high, stirring all the time and breaking up any lumps, until all the meat is sealed and browned.

Add the carrot, potatoes, tomatoes, stock and oregano and bring to the boil. Reduce the heat to medium and simmer, covered, for 12-15 minutes.

Remove from the heat, stir in the parsley and season to taste before serving.

steak and fries

serves 4

Free

ready in 20 minutes

600g large potatoes, peeled and cut into long thin chips

low calorie cooking spray

salt and freshly ground black pepper

4 x 150g thin lean beef frying steaks, visible fat removed

a mixed salad, to serve

With this easy recipe you can enjoy a yummy steak dinner any night of the week – without breaking the bank! Because frying steak only takes minutes to cook, it's perfect for people with busy lives.

Preheat the oven to 200°C/Fan 180°C/Gas 6. Place the chips in a pan of lightly salted boiling water for 2 minutes, and carefully drain.

When cool, spread them onto a baking sheet lined with baking parchment in a single layer and spray with low calorie cooking spray. Season with salt and bake in the oven for 12-15 minutes or until tender and golden.

Meanwhile, heat a non-stick griddle or frying pan until smoking. Season the meat and brown each piece on both sides. Cook to your liking: 1-2 minutes on each side for rare, 2-3 minutes on each side for medium, and 3-4 minutes on each side for well done. Remove the meat from the pan and drain on kitchen paper.

Divide the steaks between four plates and serve with the fries and a mixed salad.

Trim off any excess fat before cooking the steak so you're not tempted once it's cooked.

speedy beef and vegetable stir-fry

serves 4

Free

ready in under 25 minutes

450g lean beef stir-fry strips

4 tbsp soy sauce

1 red chilli, deseeded and finely chopped

1 tsp grated root ginger

2 garlic cloves, peeled and crushed

low calorie cooking spray

400g pack stir-fry vegetables

100g shiitake mushrooms, sliced

150ml beef stock

salt and freshly ground black pepper

4 tbsp finely chopped fresh coriander

Forget the Chinese takeaway – pile your plate high with this speedy, simple-to-make stir-fry. You can vary the vegetables – courgettes, mushrooms and red peppers make a great mix. Just remember to cut them finely so they cook quickly.

In a large bowl mix the beef strips, soy sauce, red chilli, ginger and garlic together.

Spray a large non-stick wok or large frying pan with low calorie cooking spray and place over a high heat. Add the beef and stir-fry for 5 minutes until browned.

Add the stir-fry vegetables, mushrooms and stock and stir-fry for 8-10 minutes.

Remove from the heat, season and stir in the coriander. Serve immediately over cooked egg noodles, if you like.

Serve with extra Speed vegetables instead of noodles to make this sensational stir-fry ideal for **Extra Easy** SP. Make sure your stir-fry vegetable pack only includes Speed foods too.

quick lamb and vegetable biryani

This classic biryani is a festive casserole of rice and meat. If you're feeling posh, why not replace the turmeric with a few strands of saffron – the cooking aroma and taste are exceptional!

Spray a large non-stick frying pan with low calorie cooking spray and stir-fry the lamb until brown on all sides.

Add the green beans, carrot, spices and curry powder and stir-fry for 2-3 minutes.

Pour in the rice and the stock, and stir well. Bring to the boil, cover tightly with a lid, then cook for 15 minutes on a medium-low heat or until the rice is tender.

Stir through the spinach, put the lid back on the pan and leave to steam, undisturbed, for 5 minutes before serving with a little fat free natural yogurt.

> Make double the quantity of this Indian speciality — it will keep in the fridge for a couple of days or freeze for up to 1 month.

serves 4

Free

ready in 30 minutes

low calorie cooking spray

500g lean lamb leg steaks, visible fat removed, cut into bite-sized cubes

250g green beans, trimmed and cut into 2cm pieces

1 large carrot, peeled and cut into 2cm pieces

3 cardamom pods, crushed

2 cloves

½ tsp turmeric

1 cinnamon stick

1 tbsp mild curry powder

250g dried basmati rice

500ml lamb stock

50g baby leaf spinach, chopped

fat free natural yogurt sprinkled with paprika, to serve

sticky 5-spice gammon

serves 4

1 Syn per serving

ready in under 15 minutes

2 tsp Chinese 5-spice powder

4 x 175g gammon steaks, trimmed of all visible fat and cut into large bite-sized pieces

low calorie cooking spray

2 red chillies, deseeded and finely chopped

finely grated zest and juice of 1 orange

1 level tbsp clear honey

100ml chicken stock

2 tbsp dark soy sauce

pak choi, to serve

Give your gammon steaks the wow factor with a zesty Oriental-style glaze.

Filling and flavourful, this recipe makes for a good-value family-friendly meal – and best of all it's ready in 15 minutes flat! Start that clock!

Sprinkle the 5-spice powder over the gammon steaks. Spray a large, wide, non-stick frying pan with low calorie cooking spray and cook the gammon over a high heat for 2-3 minutes or until the edges are tinged brown.

Add the red chillies, orange zest and juice, honey, stock and soy sauce and simmer rapidly for 4-5 minutes or until the sauce becomes sticky and the gammon is glazed and golden with almost burnt edges.

Serve immediately with steamed pak choi and cooked egg noodles, and any pan juices poured over.

This glaze works equally well with pork or chicken.

quick chicken, spinach and tomato curry

serves 4

Free

ready in under 30 minutes

low calorie cooking spray

1 onion, peeled and finely chopped

2 tbsp madras curry powder (or mild or medium curry powder)

1 tsp ground cinnamon

8 chicken thigh fillets, skinned and cut into bite-sized pieces

400g can chopped tomatoes

200ml chicken stock

200g frozen chopped spinach, defrosted

salt and freshly ground black pepper

8 tbsp fat free natural yogurt

fresh coriander sprigs, to garnish

A curry in a hurry, this speedy spicy chicken dish is perfect for people who love Indian cooking but don't have time to slave over a hot stove. If you're not keen on spinach use extra chopped tomatoes.

Spray a deep, lidded non-stick frying pan with low calorie cooking spray and place over a high heat.

Add the onion and stir-fry for about 2-3 minutes, then stir in the curry powder and ground cinnamon and stir-fry for 1 minute.

Add the chicken pieces and the tomatoes, stock and spinach, cover and cook for 15-20 minutes until cooked through. Season well and remove from the heat.

Stir in the yogurt, garnish with the coriander sprigs and serve with boiled white rice.

This sauce makes a great basis for any type of curry — adjust the amount of curry powder to taste and try with pork, fish, prawns or different vegetables.

lemon and garlic chicken with a warm potato salad

serves 4

Free

ready in 20-25 minutes

4 x 150g skinless and boneless chicken breasts

salt and freshly ground black pepper

finely grated zest of 1 unwaxed lemon

1 tbsp chopped fresh rosemary leaves

4 garlic cloves, peeled and very finely chopped

1 large egg white

500g new potatoes, peeled and cut into small cubes

300g green beans, trimmed and halved

200g cherry tomatoes, halved

4 tbsp fat free vinaigrette

lemon wedges, to serve

It's easy to fall in love with this simple recipe which transforms plain chicken into something spectacular in 25 minutes. You can use lean pork steaks or turkey steaks in place of the chicken.

Place the chicken breasts between sheets of cling film and, using a mallet or rolling pin, beat lightly until about 1.5cm thick. Remove the cling film and season well.

Mix together the lemon zest, chopped rosemary and garlic and spread over the chicken breasts.

Preheat the grill to medium and line the grill pan with foil. Beat the egg white on a plate with a little salt and pepper until frothy. Dip the chicken in the egg white and place on the grill pan. Grill for 10-12 minutes or until browned and crisp, turning once.

Meanwhile, boil the potatoes in lightly salted water for 10 minutes, adding the green beans for the final 3 minutes, then drain. Toss the potatoes, green beans and cherry tomatoes with the vinaigrette and season.

Divide the potato salad between four plates then serve with the chicken and lemon wedges to squeeze over.

teriyaki chicken
and vegetable stir-fry

serves 4

1½ Syns per serving

ready in under 15 minutes

3 x 150g skinless and
boneless chicken breasts,
cut into thin strips

1 tbsp dark soy sauce

low calorie cooking spray

2 carrots, peeled and
cut into matchsticks

1 red pepper, deseeded and
cut into thin strips

100g mangetout,
halved lengthways

100ml teriyaki sauce

Take your tastebuds to the Orient with a delicious stir-fry that's quick and easy to prepare.

Marinated in soy sauce and complemented with a dash of teriyaki, this tender juicy chicken is rich in authentic Japanese flavours. The crunchy vegetables add texture and colour to the dish making it a real feast for the eyes – and the stomach!

Place the chicken in a glass bowl with the soy sauce and toss to coat well.

Spray a large non-stick wok or frying pan with low calorie cooking spray and place over a high heat. Add the chicken mixture and stir-fry for 2-3 minutes.

Add the vegetables and stir-fry for 3-4 minutes.

Pour in the teriyaki sauce and stir-fry for 2-3 minutes or until piping hot before serving.

seared turkey escalopes
with sage, lemon and bacon

serves 4

Free

ready in under 15 minutes

4 x 175g turkey escalopes

salt and freshly ground black pepper

4 back bacon rashers, visible fat removed

4 large fresh sage leaves

4 slices lemon

low calorie cooking spray

200ml chicken stock

The bright flavours of lemon and sage transform simple poultry instantly.

Super-filling, super-tasty and ready in less time than it takes to heat up a ready meal, this succulent turkey dinner is a treat for the whole family.

Put each turkey escalope between two pieces of cling film and, using a rolling pin, roll them out to a thickness of about 5mm. Remove the cling film and season well.

Lay a rasher of bacon on top of each escalope and put a sage leaf on top of that. Cover the sage leaf with a slice of lemon and secure everything with a cocktail stick.

Spray a large non-stick frying pan with low calorie cooking spray. Cook the escalopes for about 3-4 minutes on each side or until golden brown and cooked through. Remove from the pan, cover and keep warm.

Add the stock to the pan and bubble until thickened and reduced by about half. Season, pour over the escalopes and serve with mashed potatoes and green beans.

You can also make this with chicken fillets. Cut a deep horizontal slit in the side of the fillet, open it out like a book then roll it out as above.

turkey, lemon
and bay leaf skewers

Easy to prepare and quick to cook, these skewers are livened up with chilli and lemon. They can be cooked under the grill, on a griddle or on the barbecue.

They make a tasty main course served with salad or work well as a starter.

Preheat the grill to medium-high and line the grill pan with foil.

On a metal skewer place one bay leaf, one lemon wedge and one turkey piece and repeat twice. Divide the remaining bay leaves, lemon wedges and turkey pieces between another seven skewers.

Place all eight skewers on the prepared grill rack.

Mix the lemon juice, dried parsley, oregano, garlic salt and red chilli flakes together. Brush this mixture over the skewers and place them under the grill for 3-5 minutes, about 14cm from the heat.

Turn the skewers, brush with more of the lemon mixture and grill for another 3-5 minutes or until the turkey is cooked through.

Serve the turkey skewers warm or at room temperature with a mixed salad.

serves 4

Free

ready in under 15 minutes

24 bay leaves

2 unwaxed lemons, cut into 24 small wedges

600g skinless turkey breast steaks, cut into 24 bite-sized pieces

juice of 1 lemon

1 tbsp dried parsley

1 tsp dried oregano

2 tsp garlic salt

1 tsp dried red chilli flakes

a mixed salad, to serve

Use chicken or lean pork instead of turkey if you fancy a change. You can also swap the lemons for limes for a subtly different flavour.

Fish in a flash

Enjoy a taste of the ocean
in record time.

parma ham wrapped cod
with sweetcorn and asparagus

serves 4

1 Syn per serving

ready in 20-25 minutes

salt and freshly ground
black pepper

4 x 175g thick skinless
cod fillets

1 tbsp finely chopped
fresh rosemary

1 tbsp finely grated
unwaxed lemon zest

8 slices Parma ham

200g asparagus tips

200g baby sweetcorn,
halved lengthways

low calorie cooking spray

In this sophisticated dish the cod is perfectly complemented by the intense flavour of Italian ham.

Ready in minutes and guaranteed to impress, this will wow guests at your next dinner party!

Preheat the oven to 200°C/Fan 180°C/Gas 6. Season the cod well.

Mix the rosemary and lemon zest together and sprinkle over the fish. Wrap each fillet with two slices of Parma ham.

Transfer to a non-stick roasting tin in a single layer and scatter the vegetables around. Spray lightly with low calorie cooking spray and place in the oven.

Roast for 12-15 minutes or until the fish is firm to the touch and the vegetables are just tender, but still retaining a slight bite.

Divide the vegetables between four plates and top with the wrapped fish.

If you prefer, you can use sustainable skinless pollack fillets instead of cod.

roasted haddock with courgettes and shallots

serves 4

Free

ready in 20 minutes

salt and freshly ground
black pepper

4 x 175g thick skinless
haddock fillets

1 courgette, cut
into 1.5cm dice

4 shallots, peeled and
finely chopped

2 tomatoes, finely chopped

a small handful of fresh
tarragon leaves, finely
chopped

low calorie cooking spray

50g wild rocket leaves

This colourful recipe works really well as a family dinner or when you're entertaining guests. For a change, add diced peppers and aubergines along with the tomatoes and courgettes and substitute the tarragon with basil for a real Mediterranean treat.

Preheat the oven to 220°C/Fan 200°C/Gas 7. Season the fish all over and place in a single layer on a non-stick baking tray lined with baking parchment.

Mix the rest of the ingredients (except the rocket) together and season well.

Spoon over the fish fillets, spray with low calorie cooking spray and cover with foil.

Roast for 12-15 minutes or until the fish is cooked through.

Spoon the vegetable mixture and juices over the fish fillets, scatter with rocket and serve immediately.

You can use any thick, skinless fish fillets for this dish or even large raw king or tiger prawns.

moroccan
halibut stew

serves 4

Free

ready in 20-25 minutes

low calorie cooking spray

1 shallot, peeled and
finely chopped

2 garlic cloves, peeled
and chopped

400g can cherry tomatoes

a pinch of saffron threads

3 or 4 sprigs of thyme

1 tsp Ras-el-Hanout or
Moroccan spice blend

400ml fish stock

800g halibut fillets,
cut into 4cm pieces

salt and freshly ground
black pepper

6 tbsp finely chopped fresh
flat-leaf parsley

lemon wedges, to serve

This recipe uses a spice blend called Ras-el-Hanout which means "top of the shop" in Arabic as a merchant's best spices would go into it. This can be found in most large supermarkets but you can use a Moroccan spice blend instead.

Spray a large non-stick frying pan or wok with low calorie cooking spray and add the shallots, garlic, tomatoes, saffron, thyme and Ras-el-Hanout or Moroccan spice blend and stir to mix well.

Add the fish stock and bring to the boil.

Reduce the heat to medium, add the fish pieces and stir gently to mix well. Cover and simmer for 8-10 minutes or until the fish is cooked through.

Remove the thyme sprigs and season well. Sprinkle with the chopped parsley and serve immediately with lemon wedges to squeeze over.

Great served
with couscous.

grilled mackerel with chilli, orange, lemon and watercress

It's recommended that we eat at least one serving of oily fish a week, as it's an excellent source of omega-3 fatty acids. And there's no tastier way of doing it than with this mackerel dish. The orange salad complements the fish perfectly.

serves 4

Free

ready in under 20 minutes

1 tsp crushed black peppercorns

2 tsp ground coriander

1 tbsp finely grated unwaxed lemon zest

4 oranges

1 red chilli, deseeded and finely chopped

8 mackerel fillets (not smoked)

2 tbsp chopped fresh coriander

110g watercress

1 small red onion, peeled and thinly sliced

Preheat the grill to high. Mix the black peppercorns, ground coriander and lemon zest together in a bowl. Grate the zest from half an orange and stir into the coriander mixture with half the chopped red chilli.

Lightly cut the skin of the mackerel and press the mixture onto the fish. Place the mackerel on a grill rack and grill, skin-side up, for 5 minutes or until crisp and cooked through. Sprinkle with the chopped coriander.

Meanwhile, segment the oranges. First slice the top and bottom off each orange, then cut away the peel and any white pith using a small, sharp knife. Cut down either side of each segment to release it.

Divide the watercress between four plates and scatter with the orange segments, sliced red onion and remaining chilli. Serve with the grilled mackerel.

This is delicious served with baby new potatoes.

salmon parcels
with fennel, tomatoes and leek

serves 4

1 Syn per serving

ready in under 30 minutes

4 x 175g skinless
salmon fillets

1 fennel bulb, finely diced

2 ripe tomatoes, finely
chopped

1 baby leek, finely chopped

salt and freshly ground
black pepper

4 tsp Pernod (or any other
aniseed liqueur)

4 slices lemon

2 courgettes, diced

1 shallot, peeled and diced

100ml vegetable stock

Anticipate a house full of enticing aromas when you spruce up your salmon fillets with this colourful vegetable mix. Baking salmon to perfection in parchment paper keeps it moist, juicy and full of flavour – and best of all it saves on washing-up!

Preheat the oven to 240°C/Fan 220°C/Gas 9. Cut four large squares of baking parchment (or aluminium foil) and place a salmon fillet in the centre of each.

Mix together the fennel, tomatoes and leek and season well. Divide the fennel mixture between the salmon fillets.

Add 1 teaspoon of Pernod to each portion and top with a slice of lemon. Fold the parchment over to completely enclose the fish. Place on a baking tray and bake in the oven for 15-20 minutes.

Meanwhile, place the courgettes, shallot and stock in a large saucepan. Place over a medium heat and simmer for 10 minutes until cooked through. Keep warm.

Remove the fish parcels from the oven and serve with the sautéed courgettes. This is delicious served with couscous.

Serve with extra Speed vegetables rather than couscous to make this meal perfect for **Extra Easy** SP.

grilled tuna with sugar snap peas and red pepper salsa

Easy enough for a weeknight and special enough for company, these tuna steaks cook up quickly on a griddle or under the grill.

To save even more time you can make your salsa up to a day before and store in the fridge until needed.

Cook the sugar snap peas in a large saucepan of lightly salted boiling water for 4-5 minutes.

Meanwhile, make the salsa by mixing all the salsa ingredients together. Season well and set aside.

Season the tuna steaks and spray with low calorie cooking spray.

Heat a non-stick ridged griddle until smoking hot, add the tuna steaks and cook for 2-3 minutes on each side or until cooked to your liking.

Drain the peas and serve immediately with the tuna steaks, red pepper salsa and boiled rice, if you like.

serves 4
Free
ready in under 20 minutes

500g sugar snap peas, trimmed

salt and freshly ground black pepper

4 x 200g tuna steaks

low calorie cooking spray

for the salsa

300g bottled Peppadew Mild Peppers, drained, rinsed and finely chopped

2 tbsp capers

finely grated zest and juice of 1 large unwaxed lemon

2 garlic cloves, peeled and crushed

2 tbsp each of finely chopped fresh coriander, mint and parsley

1 small red onion, peeled and finely chopped

Serve with extra Speed vegetables instead of rice to make this into a great Extra Easy *SP* meal.

asian-style crab with rice noodles

serves 4

½ **Syn** per serving

ready in under 15 minutes

250g dried rice noodles

200g stringless beans, thinly sliced

200g baby sweetcon, halved lengthways

400g fresh white crab meat (or 2 x 170g cans white crab meat, drained)

2 x small packs fresh coriander, finely chopped

small pack fresh mint, finely chopped

juice of 2 limes

1 level tbsp sweet chilli sauce

4 tbsp light soy sauce

1 tbsp Thai fish sauce (nam pla)

3 spring onions, finely sliced

1 red chilli, deseeded and very finely chopped

lime wedges, to serve

Good Asian food aims to balance textures and tastes with vibrant exotic colours – and this recipe does that in style.

If you prefer, you can swap the crab meat for large cooked prawns.

Place the noodles in a wide bowl, cover with boiling water and set aside for 4-5 minutes.

Meanwhile, cook the beans and baby sweetcorn in a saucepan of lightly salted boiling water for 3-4 minutes. Drain well and place in a serving bowl.

Rinse the noodles with cold water, drain thoroughly and add to the vegetables.

Add the crab meat to the bowl, along with the coriander, mint and lime juice.

Mix together the sweet chilli sauce, soy sauce, fish sauce, spring onions and chopped red chilli. Pour over the crab and noodle mixture.

Toss all the ingredients together and serve with lime wedges to squeeze over.

> Because rice noodles are easy to overcook, it's a good idea to plunge them into a bowl of cold water as soon as they're cooked and then thoroughly drain again.

prawn and vegetable stir-fry

serves 4

½ **Syn** per serving

ready in 12-15 minutes

low calorie cooking spray

1 red chilli, deseeded
and diced

2 garlic cloves, peeled
and finely chopped

2 x 250g packs
stir-fry vegetables
(Speed foods only)

salt and freshly ground
black pepper

5 tbsp vegetable stock

2 tbsp red wine vinegar

6 tbsp dark soy sauce

1 level tbsp sweet
chilli sauce

500g cooked and peeled
tiger prawns

Heat things up a bit with this chilli and garlic prawn stir-fry. As it uses ready-prepared stir-fry vegetables, this speedy meal saves you time chopping and shredding – just choose whatever selection of stir-fry veg takes your fancy at the supermarket.

Spray a large non-stick wok or frying pan with low calorie cooking spray and place over a high heat.

Add the red chilli, garlic and stir-fry vegetables, season to taste and stir-fry for 2-3 minutes.

Stir in the stock, red wine vinegar, dark soy sauce and sweet chilli sauce and cook until bubbling.

Finally add the prawns and stir-fry for 1-2 minutes or until heated through. Serve hot.

This recipe also works well with thin strips of chicken, beef or pork. Just stir-fry until cooked through before adding the chilli, garlic and vegetables.

Veggie delights

Quick, big flavoured vegetable mains and sides to tempt all tastebuds!

asparagus frittata and wedges

serves 4

2½ Syns per serving

ready in 30 minutes

6 large baking potatoes, cut into thick wedges

low calorie cooking spray

400g asparagus spears

6 large eggs

50g freshly grated Parmesan cheese

2 tbsp chopped fresh chives

1 tbsp chopped fresh oregano leaves

salt and freshly ground black pepper

passata with onion and garlic, to serve

This Italian omelette makes a quick and easy lunch or supper, made even faster and easier by cooking in a covered pan. It's equally delicious served hot or cold and makes great picnic food.

Sliced courgettes or fine green beans are good alternatives to asparagus.

Preheat the oven to 200°C/Fan 180°C/Gas 6. Bring a large pan of water to the boil and add the potato wedges. Boil for 4-5 minutes. Drain in a colander, and leave to dry for 10 minutes.

Return the wedges to the dry saucepan, cover with a lid and shake to 'rough-up' the edges – doing this will help make the wedges really crispy.

Place the wedges in a single layer on a baking sheet lined with baking parchment. Spray with low calorie cooking spray and bake for 15-20 minutes, or until golden.

Meanwhile, snap the asparagus and discard the woody ends. Lay the spears flat in a wide pan of simmering lightly salted water, or steam over boiling water, and remove after 4-5 minutes when tender but still bright green. Drain and cool under running water.

Lightly beat the eggs in a bowl, then add the asparagus, half of the grated Parmesan, the chives and oregano. Season and stir well.

Spray a 25cm lidded non-stick frying pan with low calorie cooking spray. Pour in the egg mixture and cook gently for 3 minutes, drawing back the edges with the tip of a knife and tipping the runny egg over the edges to help it set.

Cover the pan and leave over a gentle heat for 5 minutes or until set on top. Slide on to a serving plate, scatter with the remaining Parmesan, and cut into wedges.

Serve immediately with the wedges and a bowl of passata.

baked eggs
with leeks

serves 4

Free

ready in under 25 minutes

low calorie cooking spray

8 baby leeks, finely chopped

2 orange or red peppers, deseeded and finely chopped

2 garlic cloves, peeled and finely chopped

50ml vegetable stock

salt and freshly ground black pepper

4 large eggs*

2 tbsp finely chopped fresh flat-leaf parsley

*Pregnant women, the elderly and babies are advised not to eat raw or partially cooked eggs.

A traditional French way to enjoy eggs, this dish is easy to make, takes barely any preparation time and tastes absolutely delicious.

Enjoy it for brunch, as a light lunch with a Free salad or as a starter.

Preheat the oven to 230°C/Fan 210°C/Gas 8. Spray a large non-stick frying pan with low calorie cooking spray and place over a high heat.

Add the leeks, peppers and garlic and stir-fry for 2-3 minutes.

Add the stock and cook for 2-3 minutes or until the vegetables are starting to soften. Season well and spoon the mixture into four large individual ramekins or pie dishes or one medium-sized, shallow ovenproof dish.

Make a well with a spoon in the centre of each ramekin (or four wells if using one medium-sized dish) and crack an egg into each well. Season each egg and sprinkle over the parsley.

Place in the oven and cook for 8-10 minutes or until the eggs are just set or cooked to your liking. Serve immediately. This is delicious with a crisp green salad.

Use small, baby leeks if possible, as they're sweeter and more tender.

cheesy broccoli bake

serves 4

4 Syns per serving

❄ Ⓥ

ready in 30 minutes

500g broccoli florets

8 spring onions, finely chopped

200g cherry tomatoes, halved or quartered

2 large eggs, beaten

200g low fat natural cottage cheese

3 garlic cloves, peeled and crushed

salt and freshly ground black pepper

4 tbsp finely chopped fresh flat-leaf parsley

110g reduced fat Cheddar cheese, grated

This great-value recipe turns a high-Syn family favourite into a deliciously healthy meal, topped with a tasty low fat cheesy sauce everyone will love.

Simple, satisfying and ready in under 30 minutes, this versatile dish is a midweek staple that can be made ahead and frozen for extra convenience.

Preheat the oven to 220°C/Fan 200°C/Gas 7.

Cook the broccoli in a large saucepan of lightly salted boiling water for 2-3 minutes. Drain, transfer to a bowl and set aside.

Add the spring onions and cherry tomatoes to the broccoli, mix well and spoon into an ovenproof dish.

Meanwhile, whisk the eggs in a clean bowl with the cottage cheese and garlic until smooth. Season well and add the parsley.

Pour the egg mixture over the vegetables and stir briefly to distribute the ingredients evenly. Sprinkle the cheese on top and cook in the oven for 15-20 minutes or until the mixture has just set.

Remove from the oven and serve immediately.

Cauliflower florets work equally well in this recipe. You can also swap the cottage cheese for quark if you wish — just add 1 tablespoon chopped chives before you use it.

sweet potato
and carrot tagine

In this dish, sweet and tender vegetables marry with a medley of Moroccan spices to create a succulent and syrupy stew that's deliciously rich in flavour.

This hearty dish makes a fabulous family feast, working equally well as a side dish or a main course.

Place all the ingredients (except the couscous and coriander) in a large, lidded non-stick frying pan and place over a medium heat.

Bring to the boil, reduce the heat to medium, cover and simmer gently for 15-20 minutes or until the vegetables are tender.

Season well and serve over cooked couscous, garnished with chopped coriander.

serves 4

Free

❄ Ⓥ

ready in 25-30 minutes

1 large onion, peeled and finely chopped

2 garlic cloves, peeled and crushed

1 tsp finely grated root ginger

2 tsp each of ground cumin and ground cinnamon

1 tsp each of ground coriander, turmeric and dried red chilli flakes

400g can chopped tomatoes

½ tsp sweetener

250ml vegetable stock

300g potatoes, peeled and cut into 1.5cm cubes

300g sweet potatoes, peeled and cut into 1.5cm cubes

2 large carrots, peeled and cut into 1.5cm cubes

salt and freshly ground black pepper

roughly chopped fresh coriander, to garnish

Some larger supermarkets sell a spice mix called Ras-el-Hanout which is wonderfully aromatic and even contains rose petals. It would work brilliantly in this dish — use 1 teaspoon and leave out the cumin, coriander, cinnamon and turmeric.

quick butternut squash curry

serves 4

2½ Syns per serving

ready in under 25 minutes

low calorie cooking spray

1 large onion, peeled, halved and thinly sliced

2 tbsp mild curry powder

500g butternut squash flesh, cut into small bite-sized cubes

400g can chopped tomatoes

200ml light coconut milk

salt and freshly ground black pepper

roughly chopped fresh coriander, to garnish

This is a wonderfully fragrant and gently spiced curry. You can build up the heat by using a medium or hot curry powder rather than a mild one. Pumpkin makes a great alternative to squash if you fancy a change.

Spray a large non-stick frying pan with low calorie cooking spray and place over a medium heat.

Add the onion and stir-fry over a medium heat for 2-3 minutes. Add the curry powder, butternut squash and tomatoes and stir-fry over a high heat for 2-3 minutes.

Stir in the coconut milk and bring to the boil. Reduce the heat to low, cover and simmer gently for 10-12 minutes or until the squash is just tender.

Season well, remove from the heat and garnish with chopped coriander to serve. Cooked basmati rice goes well with this dish.

Try different types of squash in this recipe — acorn, spaghetti or crown prince would all work well.

cherry tomato and basil stuffed peppers

These healthy Mediterranean-style stuffed peppers are a great all-in-one meal solution for week nights and weekends and they look great on a buffet or as a starter when friends come round.

Because you can serve them hot or cold, this is a great recipe to make in advance if you're pushed for time.

Preheat the oven to 240°C/Fan 220°C/Gas 9.

Using a small knife, cut the tops off the peppers and reserve, then scoop out the seeds. Sit the peppers on a microwaveable plate, cut-side up, and cook in the microwave on high for 5-6 minutes or until they have wilted and softened.

Meanwhile, mix the quark, garlic and basil together and season well.

Spoon half of the cherry tomatoes into the base of the peppers, then spoon the quark mixture over them.

Top with the remaining cherry tomatoes and the reserved lids, spray with low calorie cooking spray and place on a baking sheet, cut side up. Bake for 8-10 minutes. Remove and serve immediately or at room temperature, sprinkled with chopped basil and parsley.

serves 4

Free

ready in under 25 minutes

4 large red peppers

250g quark

3 garlic cloves, peeled and crushed

25g finely chopped fresh basil, plus extra to garnish

salt and freshly ground black pepper

200g cherry tomatoes, halved

low calorie cooking spray

chopped fresh flat-leaf parsley, to garnish

If you don't have a microwave you can soften the peppers by placing them in a saucepan of boiling water for 4–5 minutes.

warm puy lentil, vegetable and feta salad

This satisfying salad brings with it a real taste of the Mediterranean.

This simple budget-friendly veggie recipe is super-slimming and makes a lovely light lunch, impressive starter or a substantial supper.

Toss the tomatoes, red onion, celery, carrot, garlic and lemon juice in a bowl.

Cook the lentils for 15-20 minutes in a large saucepan of boiling water until just tender, drain and add to the bowl with the coriander. Season to taste and toss to mix well.

Scatter over the feta cheese and serve immediately.

serves 4

2½ Syns

ready in 30 minutes

250g cherry tomatoes, halved

1 small red onion, peeled and finely sliced

2 celery sticks, very thinly sliced

1 carrot, peeled and coarsely grated

1 garlic clove, peeled and crushed

juice of 1 lemon

150g dried Puy lentils

a small bunch of fresh coriander, roughly chopped

salt and freshly ground black pepper

110g reduced fat feta cheese, crumbled

Cook the lentils in advance and you'll have tea on the table in a matter of minutes.

potato mash
with fennel and dill

This flavoursome mash goes well with practically all main dishes. The smooth, sweet and fragrant flavours of fennel and dill really do add a touch of magic.

serves 4

Free

ready in under 25 minutes

800g potatoes, peeled and roughly chopped

1 large fennel bulb, finely chopped

2 garlic cloves, peeled and crushed

100ml hot vegetable stock

200g fat free natural fromage frais

salt and freshly ground black pepper

4 tbsp finely chopped fresh dill

Boil the potatoes and fennel separately in two large saucepans of lightly salted boiling water for 12-15 minutes or until tender. Drain.

Put the fennel in a food processor with the garlic and stock and blend until fairly smooth.

Transfer to a wide bowl along with the potatoes. Mash with the fromage frais until you have a light creamy mixture.

Season well and stir in the chopped dill. Serve hot.

Floury potatoes such as Maris Piper and King Edward are best for this dish as they produce a light, fluffy mash.

leek and
garden pea braise

serves 4

Free

ready in under 15 minutes

low calorie cooking spray

2 garlic cloves, peeled and finely chopped

2 large leeks, thinly sliced

250ml vegetable stock

400g frozen garden peas

2 baby cos lettuce, outer leaves removed, cut into 8 wedges

salt and freshly ground black pepper

2 tbsp finely chopped fresh mint

Sweet mild leeks, garden peas, lettuce and mint provide an explosion of fresh flavours in this gorgeous side dish.

From the vegetable rack to the table in less than 15 minutes, it's the perfect accompaniment to any main course.

Spray a medium non-stick saucepan with low calorie cooking spray and place over a high heat. Add the garlic and leeks and cook, stirring, for 4 minutes or until soft.

Add the stock and bring to the boil. Reduce the heat to low and simmer for 1-2 minutes.

Add the peas and lettuce and cook, covered, for 2-3 minutes or until tender.

Season to taste and transfer to a serving bowl. Sprinkle over the mint and serve hot.

For a change, substitute the lettuce for spinach leaves.

red cabbage, red onion
and sugar snap sauté

serves 4

½ **Syn** per serving

ready in under 15 minutes

low calorie cooking spray

1 red onion, peeled and sliced

½ medium-sized red cabbage, thinly shredded

2 garlic cloves, peeled and thinly sliced

200g sugar snap peas, trimmed

4 tbsp dark soy sauce

1 level tbsp sweet chilli sauce

1 tbsp rice vinegar

¼ tsp sweetener

This sweet-and-sour braised red cabbage stir-fry is packed with flavour and it'll get you well on your way to your five a day!

This beautiful and slimming side dish is a colourful addition to any main course, and the bright green sugar snaps make a striking contrast to the blue-violet cabbage.

Spray a large non-stick pan or wok with low calorie cooking spray and add the onion and cabbage. Stir-fry over a medium heat for 3-4 minutes or until the cabbage begins to soften but still retains a bite.

Add the garlic and sugar snap peas and stir-fry for a further 3-4 minutes.

Mix together the soy sauce, sweet chilli sauce, rice vinegar and sweetener and drizzle over the cabbage. Allow to bubble for 2 minutes and serve hot.

This speedy dish is even speedier if you use a food processor to shred and slice the cabbage and onion.

spicy sweetcorn stir-fry

Fast, fresh and full of Free veg, this vibrant dish will put the sunshine into any mealtime!

This quick way of cooking sweetcorn really helps to retain its sweet flavour and crunchy texture.

Remove the corn kernels by standing each cob on its end and, holding it firmly, use a sharp knife to slice away the kernels, cutting in as close to the cob as you can.

Spray a large non-stick frying pan or wok with low calorie cooking spray and place over a high heat.

Add the ginger and spring onions, stir briefly, then add the garlic and red chilli and stir again. Add the corn kernels.

Stir fry for 4-5 minutes then add the red peppers and soy sauce.

Check the seasoning, garnish with coriander sprigs and serve immediately with cooked rice or cooked noodles.

serves 4

Free

❄ Ⓥ

ready in under 20 minutes

4 sweetcorn cobs, husks removed

low calorie cooking spray

2cm piece root ginger, peeled and finely chopped

8 spring onions, finely sliced

2 garlic cloves, peeled and finely chopped

1 red chilli, deseeded and finely chopped

200g bottled roasted red peppers in brine, drained and roughly chopped

2 tbsp light soy sauce

salt and freshly ground black pepper

fresh coriander sprigs, to garnish

If you're really pushed for time, use tinned or frozen corn instead of fresh cobs.

warm lentils with roasted squash

serves 4

Free

ready in under 30 minutes

300g peeled and diced
butternut squash and sweet
potato

1 garlic clove, peeled
and crushed

1 tsp cumin seeds

salt and freshly ground
black pepper

low calorie cooking spray

100g dried Puy or
green lentils

2 bay leaves

1 tbsp red wine vinegar

2 tomatoes, roughly chopped

1 bunch large spring onions,
sliced

small pack fresh mint,
finely chopped

The combination of lentils, spices, herbs and roasted vegetables is widely used in Mediterranean and Middle Eastern cooking. True Puy lentils come from the Puy region of France, where the fertile volcanic soil gives the lentils a superior flavour and texture.

Preheat the oven to 220°C/Fan 200°C/Gas 7.

Place the squash and sweet potato in a roasting tin, scatter with the garlic and cumin seeds and season well. Spray with low calorie cooking spray and roast in the oven for 15-20 minutes or until softened and cooked through.

Meanwhile, place the lentils and bay leaves in a pan with enough cold water to cover generously. Bring to the boil and simmer for 10-15 minutes or until just tender. Drain, then remove and discard the bay leaves.

Place the red wine vinegar in a bowl with the tomatoes and spring onions. Add the drained lentils, mint and roasted vegetables. Toss gently together and serve warm or at room temperature.

You can use any lentils you like but the green and brown varieties work best.

char-grilled cauliflower
with lemon and garlic

serves 4

Free

ready in 15-20 minutes

1 large head of cauliflower, separated into bite-sized florets

juice of 2 lemons

2 garlic cloves, peeled and crushed

1 tbsp dried mixed herbs

salt and freshly ground black pepper

2 tbsp roughly chopped fresh flat-leaf parsley

Cauliflower is a wonderfully versatile vegetable that can take on big flavours without losing its own unique character – this recipe is proof of that!

If you haven't thought about char-grilling cauliflower, give it a try – you'll soon be hooked!

Place the cauliflower florets in a saucepan of lightly salted boiling water for 4-5 minutes. Drain and transfer to a large bowl.

Meanwhile, mix the lemon juice, garlic and dried herbs together. Pour over the cauliflower, season to taste and toss to mix well.

Heat a large griddle until smoking and char-grill the cauliflower florets for 1 minute on each side or until lightly charred at the edges.

Return the florets to the bowl and toss again. Sprinkle over the parsley and serve hot or at room temperature.

oriental pak choi with tofu and shiitake mushrooms

serves 4

½ **Syn** per serving

ready in 25 minutes

250g plain firm tofu

75ml vegetable stock

4 tbsp dark soy sauce

1 red chilli, deseeded and finely chopped

4 garlic cloves, peeled and thinly sliced

1.5cm piece root ginger, sliced into thin sticks

200g shiitake mushrooms, very thinly sliced

8 spring onions, thinly sliced

200g pak choi

low calorie cooking spray

1 tbsp each of Shaoxing rice wine and rice vinegar

½ tsp dried red chilli flakes

for the marinade

1 tbsp finely grated root ginger

1 tbsp dark soy sauce and 2 tbsp light soy sauce

4 tbsp orange juice

½ level tsp golden caster sugar

Bursting with fresh vegetables and filling enough to be a main course, this dish takes just minutes to prepare so it's great for those evenings when you're in a rush. Pak choi is widely available and makes for a quick, tasty meal.

First mix all the marinade ingredients together in a bowl.

Cut the tofu into bite-sized pieces and add to the bowl. Set aside to marinate for 8-10 minutes.

Place the stock, soy sauce, red chilli, garlic, ginger, mushrooms and spring onions in a non-stick wok over a medium-high heat and stir-fry for 5-6 minutes.

Separate the pak choi leaves, add to the wok and stir-fry for 3-4 minutes. When the leaves have wilted and the stems are cooked but still a little crunchy, remove from the heat and transfer the mixture to a serving dish.

Wipe the wok out with kitchen paper. Spray with low calorie cooking spray and place over a medium-high heat. When it starts to smoke, add the tofu pieces (reserving the marinade liquid) and stir-fry for 4-5 minutes to get it browned evenly on all sides. Take care not to break up the tofu.

Season with the rice wine and the rice vinegar. Add the reserved marinade liquid, bring to a bubble and let the liquid reduce.

Sprinkle over the chilli flakes and toss well. Spoon onto the pak choi mixture and serve hot.

Marinate the tofu overnight to save time the next day.

Index

Conversions

We have used metric measurements throughout this book. If you prefer to use imperial measurements, the following lists will help you.

grams/ounces

25g	1oz
40g	1½oz
50g	2oz
60g	2½oz
75g	3oz
100g	3½oz
110g	4oz (¼lb)
125g	4½oz
150g	5oz
175g	6oz
200g	7oz
225g	8oz (½lb)
250g	9oz
275g	10oz
300g	11oz
350g	12oz (¾lb)
375g	13oz
400g	14oz
425g	15oz
450g	16oz (1lb)
500g	18oz (1lb 2oz)
600g	22oz (1lb 6oz)
800g	28oz (1lb 12oz)
900g	32oz (2lb)
1000g/1kg	36oz (2lb 4oz)

millilitres/fluid ounces/pints

25ml	1fl oz
50ml	2fl oz
75ml	3fl oz
100ml	3½fl oz
125ml	4fl oz
150ml	5fl oz (¼ pint)
200ml	7fl oz
250ml	9fl oz
275ml	10fl oz (½ pint)
300ml	11fl oz
350ml	12fl oz
400ml	14fl oz
500ml	18fl oz
600ml	20fl oz (1 pint)
700ml	24fl oz (1¼ pints)
800ml	28fl oz (1½ pints)
1.2 litres	32fl oz (2 pints)

centimetres/inches

1.5cm	½ inch
2cm	¾ inch
2.5cm	1 inch
12cm	5 inches
14cm	5½ inches
25cm	10 inches

Meet the team

Gareth

Sunil

Katy

Beverley

Lara Mike

Kathryn

Morag

Tracy

Allison